MORNING
MEDITATIONS

A GUIDED JOURNAL TO START EACH DAY FEELING CALM AND ENERGIZED

ROCK
POINT
QUARTOKNOWS.COM

Good Morning

It is a great moment of self-awareness when you realize that spending time with yourself, quietly and truly alone, is a vital component of building a happy and healthy life. There are those who find this time at night, as there is peace in the darkness when the world is still and comforting. But it is also equally beneficial to start your mornings with these moments of solace, too.

When the light starts to break through—whether brilliant sun or a cool brightness—is the moment for newness. A new day ushers in a reset, a chance to begin again. Maybe today is when you start a new exercise routine or begin a new job in a new place. Maybe your fresh start is something more subtle and internal, like choosing to see the glass half full instead of half empty. Whatever your journey, taking time to acknowledge it and set intentions first thing in the morning will set you up for an amazing day.

Consider these moments alone in the morning your time for meditation, a practice that has multiple benefits. Morning meditation enhances your awareness, helps to temper stress and anxiety, builds focus, boosts overall well-being, and sets a tone of calm for the entire day ahead.

Starting each day with an open mind is invigorating, and also helps you kick things off on a bright note and to see the big picture more clearly. So when someone greets you with Good morning! you can genuinely respond back, 'Yes, it is.'

Peaceful Intentions for Joyful Days

This journal contains meditations meant to be done at the beginning of your day, in the first precious moments you have all to yourself. Each meditation is followed by an accompanying question or reflection exercise for you to answer, writing down your responses as you go. Some of these prompts ask you to plan for the future, while others revisit the past, but all are meant to enable you to meet each day head-on with energy and purpose.

These prompts call for self-examination and intention setting, and are organized by the four seasons—spring, summer, fall, and winter. Mornings look and feel different, depending on the time of year, so it's only fitting that the way you greet them is unique as well. When the air is cool and the sun inviting, you might feel more energized and happy to start your day. But when the world outside your bed is balmy and humid or downright frigid, you might not be so eager.

It is ok to feel anything and everything fully and use these feelings to determine the path of your day. Let positive thoughts propel you with a sense of empowerment; allow less than positive thoughts to be a source of encouragement to do and be better. A joyful life begins when you welcome each and every feeling, the good and the not so great, and except them all as part of you, the pieces that make you unique and whole.

This journal embraces and encourages all that you are. Each morning that you visit the meditations here will be a new start, a new chance to discover more and more of what drives you.

Spring

What "seeds" have you planted that you need to nurture and be attentive to?

When things don't seem
to be going the way you want, you
have a choice to make: resist or welcome
peace. Resisting causes stress and anxiety.
Most of us tend to dwell on how we want things
to go and become stressed out. But if you release
control, you allow what needs to happen to play
out as it's supposed to. Many factors are at work
and we can't know how it all fits together yet.
Choose to cease resisting and allow
peace to enter.

Where in your life do you need to let go and let things happen naturally?

A morning ritual is a great way to begin each day. It is essential to your self-care to take time to create space for yourself. A ritual can be as long or as short as you like. In time, your morning routine will become a habit. With consistency, you will find a sense of motivation and calm because you are taking time to set yourself up for success every day.

List the things that must happen for you to feel your best.

Rain is a symbol of
washing away the old so that
growth can occur. Rain cleanses and
nourishes as well as destroys. Depending on
the force and timing, rain can be a welcomed
friend or a feared enemy. Nature is full of duality.
What can seem good to some can be bad to
others. It's all about the meaning we attribute
to something. The same can go for our
words and deeds. Choose to live
life with the best intentions and
offer nourishment instead
of negativity.

When do you find yourself at a crossroads with your words?

Slow down. Don't allow yourself to fall into the trap of glorifying busy-ness. Life is intended to be savored and this moment is the most important. Notice the little things and expand your awareness. Flowers bloom for only a season; children grow up fast; and the leaves change and eventually fall. Savor what's in front of you and appreciate the moment you are in.

How can you alter your routine to ensure that you move through your day consciously?

When people pass away,
those who are left behind feel
the loss. Our energy leaves a legacy after
we pass. How does your energy leave people
feeling? We have the power to raise our
vibrations and in turn attract like energy to us.
As you go through your day, catch yourself
when your energy dips or a negative thought
surfaces. Take the time to reframe it and shift
your energy from low to high. Bring
the energy you want to receive.

What things can you do to bring your highest energy forward, especially during times when you're feeling low?

The feeling of being
enough and accepting who you
are is powerful. It can be scary to
wholeheartedly accept yourself. But that's
only because important things tend to scare
us before we do them. When you are having
difficulty accepting yourself, ask: What is
one thing I can do today to accept myself?
Reframe the thoughts that deny
self-approval and cultivate
self-love step by step.

What are some small acts you can do daily that will move you
toward full self-love?

Striving for balance can
feel like an uphill battle, one that
never reaches a summit. As we strive
to balance life, we often become even more
imbalanced. There will be times when certain
areas in our lives demand more attention
than others. When this happens, instead of
stressing out about balance, strive to bring
grace and understanding to the situation and
the process. Life has ups and downs.
Bless the highs and lows: they
are what make life such a
magnificent journey.

List out the different areas of your life that demand your attention, and note what you are grateful for in each.

Think about your favorite
place in nature and how it makes
you feel. It's important to feed our souls
by removing ourselves from everyday
life and connecting with our inner animal.
Each of us has a spirit that is awakened by
being in nature. Enable your wild side to be
nurtured by its innate need to be in a
natural environment. The mountains,
desert, ocean, hills, lakes,
and trees are calling.

Where in nature will you go to awaken your spirit?

Allow yourself the space each
day to find wonder in the ordinary.
We are likely to go through our days on
autopilot and forget to notice what's around.
Sometimes we even forget to breathe. Take time
to do your activities mindfully. Notice what
your senses take in as you do the activity.
Take your time and go from mindless
to mindful. When we look for wonder,
it's amazing how it reveals itself.

Write out your to-do list for today. Then see if you can find some wonder in each task.

When you feel yourself
caught in a trap of comparing yourself
to others, take a moment to breathe and
connect with your heart. There is no one else
like you. Everyone is on their own journey
and it's not fair to compare yourself to their
distinctive path. Remind yourself of where
you want to be headed and move toward your
objectives. By keeping your eyes on
your goals, the perception of what
others are doing will become
less important.

Write down three personal goals that are unique to your journey for today, this week, this month, and this year.

Freedom comes through forgiveness. When we hold on to hurt, our hearts and minds fill with negativity, which slowly eats away at our spirit. Forgive those who hurt you and release any pain, resentment, or bitterness that has taken root. Allow freedom to pass through you. Let go of the need to control the outcome and people's reactions. Don't continue to suffer long after the pain occurred. Choose to forgive over and over so that freedom and love can return.

Who do you need to forgive today?

True vibrancy comes from within. The light in our eyes, the radiance in a smile, the glow of our skin are all manifestations of how we take care of ourselves inwardly. Spiritual health is just as important as physical health. Take some time each day to find your light. Breathe in your brilliance, breathe out the chaos. When we access our light, we can feel our inner power expand. When you glow from within, you are magnetic.

What acts of self-care can you practice daily to brighten your glow both inside and out?

Rise like the sun: awaken each part of your body gently, intentionally, and slowly. Feel your breath fill your lungs, sending oxygen to your extremities. Let your senses come alive, sending energetic vibrations throughout your body. Take in the sights and sounds of the morning with deep awareness. Take your time as you move through your morning. Greet the day from a place of gentleness as you gradually develop a routine.

What tasks can you insert into your routines that will smooth the rough edges of the daily grind and create a sense of lightness?

A rose blooms in a pattern of perfection. Each petal has a place and unfolds with perfect timing. As the blossom unfurls, it releases an intoxicating scent. The scent of the rose carries the highest vibrational scent and elevates the mood of those who stop to smell it. If you pass by a rosebush today, stop. Take the time to infuse your day with high vibrations just by smelling a flower. This mindful act will elevate your mood and add positivity to your day.

What other smells and scents instantly lift your mood when you're
feeling down?

In the beginning of
something new, we feel excitement.
It brings our awareness to possibility,
hope, and even creativity. When we begin,
anything is possible. The shape of something
new is limitless. Every morning we have the
opportunity to see the day this way. We can
choose to see the hope of beginning and
allow our creativity to shape the day we
desire. When we choose creativity over
comfort, our day becomes brighter
and more exciting.

How can you be creative today?

Summer

This is the season of revitalization and strength.

Rise like the sun: awaken each part of your body gently, intentionally, and slowly. Feel your breath fill your lungs, sending oxygen to your extremities. Let your senses come alive, sending energetic vibrations throughout your body. Take in the sights and sounds of the morning with deep awareness. The warmth of the summer sun permeates everything it encounters. It creates energy and growth. The days are longer as the sun lingers, glistening deep into the evening. When you express warmth and emit energy, you leave a lasting impression with everyone you encounter. Your energy speaks volumes. Wild and free, the one who embrace life with joy. Peaceful and serene, the one who find time to be quiet and still. Joyful and creative, the one who open their minds to possibility and growth. You are all of these things.

Life is truly amazing!
Just think about all you've gone
through to get where you are right now.
You've had many milestones and made
several decisions to get here. You have
accomplished so many things and have made
an impact on various lives. Even the things
that felt like mistakes brought you
to this moment, which is exactly
where you're meant to be. You have
a full day ahead of you.

How will you add to the story of your life?

We all want to belong
and feel accepted. There is a spark inside
you that makes you unique. People are lucky
to know you. Take down the walls you've
built to protect your heart. If you've been hurt
before, release the pain of those memories
and do the work to mend the place where the
wound began. Not everyone is supposed to
stay in our lives, but the ones who stay are
worthy of our hearts. Open your heart
to those people. Love and acceptance
are on the other side of the wall.

Make a plan for how you can bring down any remaining walls to ensure that you don't miss out on anyone or anything.

In a garden, food grows from a tiny seed. Some plants make their way to the surface and grow in plain sight, while others stay underground, showcasing only their greenery. No matter where they grow, they offer nutrition and sustenance. Sometimes our personal growth is outward for all to see and other times it is hidden from sight. You are always growing. Even when there isn't physical evidence, growth is inevitable.

In what ways are you growing, both inward and outward?

Choose the adventure your
life provides. Each day is a blank page,
ready to be filled with our ups and
downs, which create a beautiful story.
Even though the adventure is not always
easy, vibrancy comes through resilience,
overcoming, and the happiness that awaits
us on the other side of every trial. Each
adventure presents itself as a way to
recalibrate our light more brilliantly.

How can you frame today's events as your own personal adventure?

Start something new,
especially when you feel stuck.
Inviting newness into your life brings
joy and creativity. Take a new route to
work, try a different food, or get going on
a new project you've been thinking about
starting. Change can be scary, but also
rewarding. When we start something new,
we expand our minds and horizons.
Be open and fluid. Trust that
what is meant to enter
your life will come.

How can you create momentum in your life to invite and embrace change?

Everything in nature has
something to offer. A flower
offers pollen to the birds and bees.
The sun offers luminosity and warmth.
The snow offers water to rivers as it melts.
The rain offers relief to the parched Earth.
Think about how you serve others and
show up each day. If you aren't using
your talents, find a way to implement
them into your life. Walk into your
strength and own your power.

Your offering is your present to the world. What is it for today?

Freedom comes from the truth,
but the truth is not always easy to speak
or even live. Our truth can be uncomfortable
for others, but if not expressed can cause us
the greatest discomfort. When we live in our
truth, we feel lighter and free. Even if admitting
the truth is tough, the weight lifted from
speaking it is worth our effort. Choose
freedom over comfort.

What is something you need to express, and how can you
acknowledge your truth?

In a forest, all forms of life support one another. The soil provides nutrients for the plants and trees, which provide shade, oxygen, and food for the animals. Even the animals provide important nutrients and help control overgrowth. Everything works in a precious equilibrium. Nature intuitively knows what it needs to thrive, just as your intuition knows what you need. Spend some time in silence this morning to tap into your inner wisdom. Everything you need is within; create space for the answers to be revealed.

What do you need in order to be supported and to be able to support others in return?

Healing comes in waves.
Sometimes we feel as if we're
drowning in sorrow. At other times
it feels as if we are riding a wave without
a care in the world. Don't rush your heart
to heal. Allow the swells to come. When
calm finally arrives, bless the pain and the
lessons it brought. In time you will feel
better, stronger, and more resilient. This
time is a gift. Let your heart express all
the feelings that come. You are making
room for what's meant to come.

Write about a time you were hurt. Are you able to move towards healing today?

Speak to yourself as you
would to the one you love the most.
Honor and respect your mind, body,
and soul. Take care of yourself by catching
negative self-talk and reframing self-judgments.
You deserve kindness, love, and approval.
Say something loving to yourself each morning.
With practice, your thoughts toward yourself
and others will change. Love will emit
from you powerfully and you
will become irresistible.

Write a love note to yourself for the day ahead.

Early on a summer morning,
the air may have a slight chill.
It feels crisp and refreshing right before
the heat sets in. As the Earth warms up,
flowers open to face the rising sun and the
water sparkles with the sun's reflection. Then
as night falls, the cooling begins and the cycle
continues. Everything is cyclical. Nothing is
permanent. If you are feeling stressed
about something, know that it
will pass. Breathe in strength;
you will get through this.

What stressors can you address and then exhale this morning so that you have a lighter day?

It's a mystery how we end up
in the families that we do. If you had a
difficult childhood, forgiveness and healing
are available with time. Your wounds can
be a light for others in similar situations.
Healing takes strength and your soul knows
its capabilities. Some of the strongest souls
heal from harsh realities. You are a
miracle and your survival is proof of
your strength and resilience.

Reflect on your childhood. Are there any amends that you are due or need to make to members of your family?

When things are uncomfortable,
it's easy to give up and walk away. If we
never push past our discomfort, we will never
find the understanding and wisdom that awaits
us on the other side. Discomfort is a gift. It brings
a deeper meaning to life. The growth that occurs
after a period of difficulty leads to resilience
and empathy. Choose to see discomfort as
a gift to help others and not as a burden.
We become polished through
pressure, not ease.

What uncomfortable conversations might you need to have with others, and what good can you hope they will bring?

Each of our friends were once strangers. Think about each person in your life who has made a difference. These people were once unknown and eventually, you created a bond of trust and love with each of them. Every person we meet has the possibility to impact our lives in a positive way. Treat each stranger with love and respect as you never know where an interaction may lead. Keep your heart and mind open to the possibilities.

Has anyone new recently entered your life that you can see becoming a friend? How will you work to grow this friendship in love and respect?

Holding space for another
person requires active listening
through presence and respect. When
people share their stories, they are inviting
you in with a bid for connection. Giving them
the time and space to express themselves is an
offering and deep connections are formed with
each interaction. We tend to get wrapped up
in our own story when we need to listen.
Try to really hear what they are saying and
offer the empathy and love they are
seeking. Open your ears when
others choose you to open
their hearts to you.

How can you be more open and receptive to the stories of others?

What is your superpower?
There are many things that we are good at and our superpower is the one thing that if we didn't do it, we would feel a void in our life. This is the thing that you're passionate about; that people come to you for. Tap into your inner power and find the things that keep you from sharing your talents. Do less of what drains your power and more of what empowers you.

What can you let go of that might be a roadblock to using
your superpower?

It's easy to get lost in distractions. The more energy we give to the things that keep us from focusing, the easier it is to stay distracted. Taking time to pay attention to what's most important to us will help us create, complete, and concentrate on our motivations.

Make a list of all the things that distract you and then a list of what needs your focus. To make progress, choose what you will give your attention to today.

Fierce determination can
bring many wonderful things into
our lives. It takes hard work and focus to
create greatness. When we put our minds
toward what we want instead of what isn't
working, we harness our potential to
make things happen. You have the
power to be the change
you want to see.

Write about your deepest desires and how you can make a move toward those desires today. Keep going until you are closer to your desired outcome.

Fall

This is the season of change and evolution.

The changes that occur in life are sometimes designed to uproot you, challenge you, and make you question whether your strength is being tested. These times are difficult, and it can feel as if there is no end in sight. But this season will end. All things come to an end. Know this: You are stronger than you give yourself credit for. You can handle hard things. When you get through this, your strength will have increased and your spirit will be more resilient. The path to success is not straight and narrow. Many diversions, doubts, and mistakes happen along the way. Milestones remind you of what you are working toward. Celebrate the small successes you achieve along the way. When confusion and fear surface, remind yourself how far you've come. Keep looking toward your objectives and make moves every day to achieve your dreams. Be flexible and adapt to change. A bird doesn't worry if it's aiming too high; it just flies by instinct. Soaring above the clouds, hovering over the oceans, birds are a symbol of freedom and perspective. When we desire freedom, we must relinquish control. To soar high, we have to let go of the limiting beliefs we hold on to because they provide the illusion of control. Step back and see the horizon, and then take a leap into freedom, allowing the higher perspective to be your guide.

After a long season of growth,
fruit is ready for harvest. It's amazing
what can grow from a tiny seed. A seed
can generate an entire bounty. With proper
care and nourishment, a plant will yield
fruit for many years. Harvest is a reward for
all the hard work and patience put into the
plant's growth. We are like plants that
go through seasons of growth,
harvest, and rest.

What season are you in right now, and how can you honor where you are in this season?

One of the most tranquil times
in a city is early in the morning. As the sun
rises, the buildings reflect their gleam, painting
the streets with a golden hue. There is a
stillness before the day begins and the streets
fill with people going their various ways. Even
in the busiest of cities, sunrise brings beauty
and the opportunity to be still and welcome
the day from a place of peace.

How will you receive peace today?

Courage is the antidote
to fear. Great things take bravery.
What are you on the verge of exploring,
creating, or otherwise doing? Think about
what your life would be like once you
achieve it. Take the doubts and fears and
breathe courage into them. One of the
first actions toward actualizing your
dreams is breathing in courage
and breathing out fear.

What is something important you want to achieve but feel scared to go after?

Worrying about the day
only invites anxiety. Today will go
exactly as it needs to go. The only thing
you can control is your reaction to the things
that happen around you. If you feel anxious
about something, spend a moment to reframe
it in your head. Turn the negative thought into
something positive and enter your day
with fresh eyes and the resolve to
react less and invite calm when
anxiety begs to thrive.

Write down three negative thoughts you have this morning, then change them to something positive.

There is power in saying no. Having too many things to concentrate on can keep you from giving your full attention to the task at hand. Place boundaries on your time and give yourself the space to breathe. Life shouldn't be lived in a vortex of stress and struggle. Review your to-do list and make note of what you can put off until later. You deserve to have space to focus, breathe, and create with a clear mind.

Review today's to-do list, and organize your tasks into Do Now and
Do Later.

Everything you have gone
through has created a mosaic, colorful
and rich. Each experience adds depth to
your life, giving you greater awareness and
understanding. You are a brave soul, and
as you overcome hardship you become a
beacon for others, glimmering hope in
dark places. Continue to spread your
brilliance; The world is a better
place with you in it.

How will you bring hope and love to those around you?

Fall is a special time of year, as the air becomes crisper and things seem cozier. Leaves are changing their colors; the temperatures drop, and the sun rises later. Harvest has been completed and part of the world is getting ready to settle into the cooler months when hibernation begins. Fall has a magical essence, with its vibrant colors, cooler air, and the completion of a season of growth.

Reflect on how you've changed this year.

Be wild and free. There is a
spirit inside of you that is primal.
Let it flow—and reach for what fills your soul.
Your intuition is the voice of your soul; listen
to what you truly desire. Release any feelings
of guilt or judgment. Allow your soul to speak
its truth. Be open to your inner truth and allow
your spirit to be your guide. Life should
be joyful and exciting. Sometimes we
need to set our primal nature free.

What are some ways you can free yourself up to hear your inner truth?

If you were to be truly honest with yourself, how would you answer the question "Am I becoming the person I want to become?" If the answer is anything but yes, dig deeper and ask yourself, "Who do I want to become?" Every day we can create the reality we desire. It doesn't always mean big sweeping changes, but it could mean choosing a different path, meal, activity, or thought.

What can you do today to bring yourself closer to whatever it is
you really want?

Life is full of obstacles
and we get to choose our paths.
Almost everything we do is by choice.
Whether we choose the right path depends
on our outlook and ability to right the
course if it seems wrong. When faced with
a decision, take some time to tap into your
intuition and find your inner compass.
You already know the answer. It lies
deep within you. Listen closely.

Write about a decision you have on the horizon, and your thoughts around how you might go about making your choice.

Think about a time when
someone offered you true empathy.
Didn't it feel comforting to be seen
and heard? Empathy is a healing emotional
balm. Being able to understand and share the
feelings of another person creates connection.
We all have times when we need to give and
receive empathy. Be present with others
and hear what they are expressing and
feeling. Offer genuine understanding.
and notice how your heart
connection grows.

How can you show empathy often with loved ones?

We all have a spark
within us. It's made up of our
charisma and energy. When we sparkle
we can illuminate an entire room. Throughout
our lives our spark waxes and wanes, like the
moon. Sometimes we feel its warmth and
other times it's hard to find. To keep your
spark alive and well, do things that
light you up. Allow yourself
to shine and be seen.

What are the things that set your soul on fire?

The pursuit of perfection is
a losing battle because nothing will
ever be perfect. Since everything is
consistently changing, it would be impossible
to try to make something permanent. We do
this with ourselves, our children, our friends, our
jobs, and even where we live. When we live in
a state of acceptance, we can come to terms
with things just as they are. There is always
room for improvement, yet perfection
is an unreasonable goal. Aim for better
and then accept what is.

What are some ways you can accept what is while also learning and growing to be better?

Fall mornings are crisp
and full of color as the leaves reveal
their true colors. The days are becoming
cooler and everything seems to be preparing
for winter's arrival. Just before the trees
become bare and the ground freezes, there
is such vibrancy to behold because for a short
while, trees are their most vibrant color.
Take the time to enjoy their stunning colors.
Notice how each tree is different, yet beautiful.
The world is full of diverse beauty.

Write about the many beautiful differences you see within the people in your life.

There's always another
side of the story or perspective
to be considered. By doing this,
we focus on compassion and empathy.
If you are facing a difficult situation with
someone, try to see it from their perspective.
This doesn't mean you have to agree; it just
allows compassion to enter and perhaps solve
some parts of the conflict. We are doing
the best we can with the tools we have.
Let go of resentment by trying to
see the other side. Imagine what
healing would occur if we all did
this for each other.

Think back to a time where a difficult situation led to an argument or resentment on your part. How could you have handled that differently?

Today is the perfect day
to show appreciation. Go through
your day with mindful gratitude for
everyone and everything. In a season of
thanksgiving, it can be easy to overgeneralize
gratitude. It is one of the most powerful
emotions and when we practice it, it can raise
our energetic vibrations. As we give thanks,
we train our brains to see the positive side
of things and of others. Give appreciation
wholeheartedly and feel your heart
send out love with each thought
or expression of thanks.

What are you most thankful for this season?

No one is exactly like you.
It's amazing to think that each one of
us is different because of our minds, bodies,
and souls. We are here with a distinct purpose
and imprint that won't be duplicated. Celebrate
what makes you different: you are special
just the way you are. Notice and celebrate
the differences in others. Find the
awe in diversity that each of us
contributes to the world.

What are your most treasured qualities that set you apart from everyone else?

The branches of an oak reach
outward and upward toward the sky.
Its branches are like tentacles—some gnarled,
others straight as if they are floating midair.
The oak always reaches for greater heights and
wider horizons. They are a spectacular sight to
behold—strong, sturdy, and expansive. Be like
the oak and never stop reaching. Always stretch
yourself further and when you think you've
reached enough, keep reaching. There's
no telling where you'll end up.

How can you extend yourself today in your work, at home, or in your relationships with others?

Concentration can seem
elusive when it feels as if all the
tabs in your brain are open. We live in an
endless loop of information. Although this is
convenient and awesome, it takes a toll on our
nervous systems. To function at our highest
capability, we need to take time for stillness.
Start your day shutting down all the tabs
in your brain and finding your center.
Let peace enter if only for a moment.
Breathe in the stillness.

Make a list of all the things you can release from your brain this morning to ensure a clear day ahead.

Winter

This is the season of peace and rest.

How sweet life can be when you allow it to be easy. Letting go of resistance and embracing the lessons that come with each struggle and reveling in victories are part of the ride. Learning to allow things to come and go can be one of the hardest lessons because we crave control. But the lesson shows us that surrendering to what is makes life richer. When you feel the urge to resist, remember that on the other side of the resistance is a new level of comfort. There is an art to doing nothing, especially with all the distractions available. It's normal to want to distract ourselves with something when nothing is exactly what we need. When you're feeling overwhelmed, tired, or overstimulated, do nothing. Sit with your thoughts. In this space, clarity can surface. In this space, your mind and spirit can reset. Happiness comes from cultivating a spirit of contentment. You are exactly where you need to be. All of the things you wish for may come, but for right now, everything you need has been provided. Look at your life knowing that everything is as it should be. Breathe in this truth and find peace knowing that all is well. Lift your arms to the sky with gratitude. Feel your heart swell with appreciation and attract happiness by choosing to be content.

As winter approaches,
notice what didn't grow this
year alongside what blossomed and
flourished. Focus on the things that thrived
and not what wilted. Release what didn't
thrive and celebrate what transpired.
This is a season to reflect, release,
and make room for what is meant to
grow in the spring. Celebrate what
grew as well as what failed.

Reflect on what has grown in your life, as well as what might not have flourished. What can you do to see a better outcome in the future.

Travel opens our minds to people and stories that we wouldn't experience at home. Our planet and fellow human beings are awesome. We can learn from so many different perspectives and see so many places. Even venturing to another town or city nearby can open our minds to something new. When we stay in our comfort zones, we don't let ourselves expand. Expansion allows magic to happen and pushes us to grow. Invite magic into your day by doing something or going somewhere different.

Make a list of ways you intend to break out of your comfort zone.

Comparison can keep us
from experiencing happiness. Where
you are right now is exactly where you
need to be. Worrying about what others
are doing takes your attention away from
the present moment. If we spend our days
comparing ourselves to others, we rob
ourselves of the opportunity to lead
a fulfilling and happy life. When you
find your mind comparing, bring it
back to the moment at hand.

Describe the things about yourself that you are glad to have.

To create a richer life, gather your
tribe and let them know how important
they are to you. Spending time with our
tribe fosters connection and understanding.
Life is designed to be shared, and when
we identify the people who make our lives
better just by being in it, we foster a sense
of belonging. A tribe can be as little or
as large as you desire. Choose those
who uplift, inspire, and interact
with a spirit of love.

What do you love about the members of your tribe, and how to do they inspire you to be better each day?

Your body is intelligent
and provides clues about what
it needs. When we are in touch with
our intuition, we can easily pay
attention to the clues our body provides.
By tapping into our inner wisdom, we
can live a healthier and more vibrant life.
Pay attention to what your body is
telling you. Make your health a priority
and show your body deep respect
and appreciation.

How will you nourish your body and mind today?

When mornings become cooler and the sun takes a bit more time to make it over the horizon, we go inward. As winter approaches, nature begins to rest. After a year of growth and producing, plants and animals slow down and store up their energy. Take the time to slow down to restore your energy. It's okay to take breaks.

How can you let go of the need to overproduce today?

You are the writer of
your story and you get to choose
the meaning you give to the events in
your life. If you allow yourself to adopt the
narrative of a victim, that is the energy
you will attract. True empowerment comes
when you choose to change the narrative
into something that helps you climb up
above the struggle and tap into
your resilience.

How are you going to rewrite your narrative and take your power
back today?

Start today with an
open heart and fresh eyes. Today
has no mistakes in it. Embrace this
clean slate by breathing in this present
moment of newness, of possibility, and of
hope. Nothing but what is happening right
now matters. Yesterday is over and
today stands before you
without expectation.

What type of energy will you choose to bring to the day?

There is nothing like a fresh
cup of coffee or tea in the morning.
It is a slow ritual to begin the day. It is
satisfying to wait for the water to brew the
grounds or tea leaves to seep to create
the perfect cup. If we can wait for perfection
in a cup each morning, why do we get so
impatient with the bigger things in life?
If you are in a period of waiting, take
a deep breath and know that
good things take time.

When you find yourself feeling impatient or rushed, what can you do to slow down and take a step back?

When you awaken, take a moment to do a scan of your body. Notice any places where tension may be and breathe into each one. Feel your breath fill you as it relieves the tension. Allow the oxygen to reach all the way to your fingers and toes. Notice how you feel after each breath. Take this bodily awareness into your day and be grateful for your body and the wonderful miracle it is to be alive.

What do you love about your body?

Waking up to a blanket
of fresh snow is a remarkable
and peaceful sight. Everything feels
cozier and the world seems hushed.
Snow is like a fresh slate, covering everything
in white. Even the soil underneath lies dormant,
waiting for the warmth of spring. It's okay
to have periods of rest. Everything needs
time to recharge. If you need stillness,
allow yourself to be still. Just as the
Earth goes through seasons,
so do our bodies. Be kind
to yourself today!

How will you make time to recharge today?

Even the smallest things
can make an impact. On the day
you were born, you changed someone's
life. You are a miracle and the world is
more lovely with you in it. Everything about
you is special, from your smile to the way you
think. Your soul is here to illuminate and
shine in its own extraordinary way.
Accept everything about yourself,
because there is no one else
quite like you.

What do you hope your lasting impact on the world will be?

In shade, ivy creeps its
way up the trunk of an olive tree.
It clings tightly to the tree, spinning its
way around the trunk. The tree does not
hinder the growth of the ivy; it just stands tall,
offering shade while staying rooted in its own
growth. If you are offering support to someone,
stay rooted in your own growth. Take time
to replenish yourself and care for your own
needs. Then you can be the supportive
person you want to be.

In what ways can you be there for those you care about without ignoring your own self-care needs?

Sometimes life feels like
being caught in a tornado. Mornings
can be especially difficult when we have
so many things to do and take care of.
But a tornado loses its power eventually.
Its centrifugal force unwinds and there
is calm after the storm. If you are feeling
wound up this morning, take the time
to unwind. Our mornings set
the tone for our day.

Instead of entering the day spinning, how can you take the extra time to find calm?

A tree sways in the
wind, its leaves dancing with
the breeze. It doesn't seem bothered
by the wind's power; it simply bends and
moves with the current. Life is full of changes,
and if we don't accept them as they come
about, we can break like branches that don't
sway with the wind. Learning to be flexible
creates acceptance of whatever life offers.
Learn to sway like a tree, to stay open
and flexible. Sometimes the
unexpected parts of life are
the most beautiful.

Reflect on a time where you were not very flexible. What are some things you can do differently next time?

After a cold night, the
ground is crystalized with a
blanket of frost. This shimmering,
icy layer can keep us from moving quickly
and rushing through our mornings. Frost is
an invitation to mindfully enter your morning
unrushed. As the ice melts, be grateful for the
warm bed you slept in and the beauty of a
winter morning. Allow gratitude to enter
if frustration may be bubbling up. Winter is
a time to rest and move slower. Take a
cue from nature and allow
the day to progress
without rushing.

Write about what you are grateful for within your daily moments of chaos.

Going through a painful
period can feel isolating. It feels
as if no one understands or knows the
right thing to say. Eventually, joy finds its
way back. It can show up in the kindness of a
friend or a gorgeous sunrise. Slowly, it creeps
back into your soul. Absorb each small moment
of joy. Those moments will become easier
to recognize and you may find yourself
blessing the pain you went through
when joy finds its way back
into your heart.

Reflect on a time when you were shown immense kindness during a painful situation. How can you pay that kindness forward to others?

Mornings provide the feeling of freshness. The air smells clean and feels like a new beginning. The dew left on the ground glistens like a shiny new object. Everything is renewed and fresh. As you awaken, feel the renewal that sleep provided. Be present with this feeling. Nothing else matters in this moment. Be here now, ready to take on the new day that has dawned. Right now is your chance to begin again. Today you have the gift of a fresh start.

What worries do you want to let go of today?

Brimming with creative inspiration, how-to projects, and useful information to enrich your everyday life, Quarto Knows is a favorite destination for those pursuing their interests and passions. Visit our site and dig deeper with our books into your area of interest: Quarto Creates, Quarto Cooks, Quarto Homes, Quarto Lives, Quarto Drives, Quarto Explores, Quarto Gifts, or Quarto Kids.

This edition published in 2022 by Rock Point, an imprint of The Quarto Group,
142 West 36th Street, 4th Floor, New York, NY 10018, USA
T (212) 779-4972 F (212) 779-6058 www.QuartoKnows.com

Contains content previously published in 2020 as *Sunrise Gratitude* and in 2021 as *Morning Meditations* by Rock Point, an imprint of The Quarto Group, 142 West 36th Street, 4th Floor, New York, NY 10018, USA.

Rock Point titles are also available at discount for retail, wholesale, promotional, and bulk purchase. For details, contact the Special Sales Manager by email at specialsales@quarto.com or by mail at The Quarto Group, Attn: Special Sales Manager, 100 Cummings Center Suite 265D, Beverly, MA 01915 USA.

10 9 8 7 6 5 4 3 2 1

ISBN: 978-1-63106-862-1

Publisher: Rage Kindelsperger
Creative Director: Laura Drew
Managing Editor: Cara Donaldson
Cover and Interior Design: Kim Winscher

Printed in China

This journal provides general information on forming positive habits and creating feelings of peace and calm. However, it should not be relied upon as recommending or promoting any specific diagnosis or method of treatment for a particular condition, and it is not intended as a substitute for medical advice or for direct diagnosis and treatment of a medical condition by a qualified physician. Readers who have questions about a particular condition, possible treatments for that condition, or possible reactions from the condition or its treatment should consult a physician or other qualified healthcare professional.